PRAC
11/03

Play
Piano
Today!

Y0-ARM-424

A Complete
Guide to
the Basics

by Warren Wiegratz and Michael Mueller

Recorded at Beat House, Milwaukee, Wisconsin

ISBN 0-634-03301-8

HAL•LEONARD® CORPORATION

7777 W. BLUEMOUND RD. P.O. BOX 13819 MILWAUKEE, WI 53213

Visit Hal Leonard Online at
www.halleonard.com

Contents

Introduction

Track 1

Welcome to *Play Piano Today!*—the series designed to prepare you for any style of piano playing, from rock to blues to jazz to classical. Whatever your taste in music, *Play Piano Today!* will give you the start you need.

About the CD

It's easy and fun to play piano, and the accompanying CD will make your learning even more enjoyable, as we take you step by step through each lesson and play each song along with a full band. Much like with a traditional lesson, the best way to learn this material is to read and practice a while first on your own, then listen to the CD. Play Piano Today! is designed to allow you to learn at your own pace. If there is ever something that you don't quite understand the first time through, go back on the CD and listen again. Every musical track has been given a track number, so if you want to practice a song again, you can find it right away.

The Basics

Posture

Track 2

Proper posture at the keyboard is an integral part of playing the piano, as poor posture can lead to neck and back soreness and wrist pain, which may adversely affect your performance. The bench should face the keyboard squarely. Sit up straight on the front half of the bench. Your arms should hang loosely from your shoulders, and your elbows should be slightly higher than the keyboard. Keep your wrists straight and your fingers curved. Your knees should be slightly under the keyboard with your feet flat on floor. Your right foot may be positioned slightly forward, as it will later be responsible for operating the foot pedals.

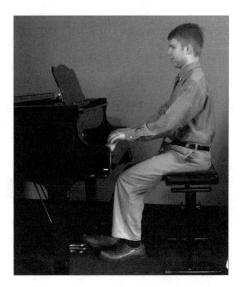

Right and Left Hand

Each finger on your right and left hands has its own number: Thumb = 1; index = 2; middle = 3; ring = 4; pinky = 5.

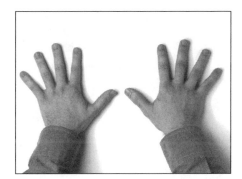

The Keyboard

The piano keyboard contains 88 keys, consisting of 52 white keys and 36 black keys. The lowest note on the piano is A, and the highest is C. The C nearest the middle of the keyboard is called "middle C."

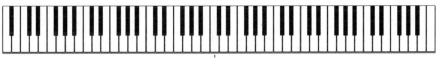

Middle C

The Right Hand

Treble Clef

Musical sounds are indicated by symbols called notes, and are found on a musical **staff**. The staff consists of five horizontal, parallel lines, and notes can be placed either on or between the lines of the staff. Notes higher on the staff are higher in pitch; notes lower on the staff are lower in pitch.

To name the notes on the staff, we use the first seven letters of the alphabet: **A–B–C–D–E–F–G**. Adding a **treble clef** assigns a particular note name to each line and space on the staff, centered around the pitch G, the second line of the staff.

The pitches on the lines of the staff (from bottom to top) are E, G, B, D, and F. An easy way to remember these is the following mnemonic: **E**very **G**ood **B**oy **D**oes **F**ine. The notes in the spaces simply spell "FACE."

Every Good Boy Does Fine

F A C E

C Position

Find middle C, and place your right-hand thumb on that note. Your right-hand index finger should fall on D, your middle finger on E, ring finger on F, and your pinky finger on G. This is called C position.

Play each note in order, one at a time, beginning with your thumb on C.

Track 3

C D E F G

Rhythm

The rhythm of a note indicates how long, or for how many beats, a note should sound. A *quarter note* is indicated by the following symbol: ♩ = one beat

Time Signature

In 4/4 time, the bottom four indicates that each beat has the duration of a quarter note, and the top four indicates that there are four quarter notes in a measure.

First Song

Track 4

Count "one–two–three–four" as you play each note.

Here is a short melody using quarter notes from the C position. First try it on your own, then listen and play along with the CD.

Second Song

Track 5

Say the note names aloud as you play (e.g., "C, D, E...").

Half Notes

A *half note* has a duration twice as long as a quarter note and is indicated by the following symbol:

half note
(2 beats)

Track 6

► Count "one, two, three, four," but remember, each half note receives two beats.

Third Song

Track 7

Five-Note Song

Track 8

I'm Calling

The Left Hand

Bass Clef

The notes played with the left hand are notated on the musical staff with a **bass clef**, which assigns the note names centered around F. The notes on the lines in bass clef are G, B, D, F, and A, and can easily be remembered as **G**ood **B**oys **D**o **F**ine **A**lways. The notes in the spaces are A, C, E, and G, and those can be remembered using **A**ll **C**ows **E**at **G**rass.

Good   Boys   Do   Fine   Always

All   Cows   Eat   Grass

C Position

Find the C note one octave below middle C (moving left on the keyboard, the next C after middle C), and place your left-hand pinky finger there. Your ring finger falls on D, middle finger on E, index finger on F, and your thumb on G.

Now, play each note, one at a time, beginning with your pinky finger on C, and try saying the note names aloud as you play them to help you memorize where they are on the staff.

Track 9

Here is a bass melody using quarter and half notes with a repeat sign. Practice playing it by yourself, and then play along with the CD track. Don't forget to count!

Lefty Lucy

Track 10

Say the note names aloud as you play.

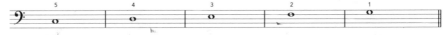

9

Whole Notes

The whole note receives four beats in 4/4 time. It is twice the duration of a half note, and four times the duration of a quarter note.

whole note

o = 𝅗𝅥 + 𝅗𝅥 = ♩ ♩ ♩ ♩
(4 beats)

Track 11

Dance with Me

Track 12

Go Find the Roadie

Rests

In addition to notes, songs may also contain silences, or rests—beats in which you play nothing at all. A rest is a musical pause. Just like notes, rests have rhythmic values that instruct you how long (or how many beats) to pause: quarter, half, and whole rests.

whole rest
(four beats)

half rest
(two beats)

quarter rest
(one beat)

Here is a one-note exercise for you to become accustomed to playing with rests. Count aloud, inserting the word "rest" on any beat that it appears. For example, the first measure should be counted: One, two, rest, four.

Track 13

Rest Easy

Stop Right There

Track 14

Now, let's try a simple right-hand melody. Again, count along, inserting the word "rest" where appropriate.

Track 15

You're Under A Rest

Metronome

Using a metronome is a practice tool that provides a rhythmic pulse to help you keep time. The tempo on a traditional, mechanical pendulum model ranges from 40 to 208 beats per minute. New digital models can go even faster. When learning a new song, you can set the tempo to a level at which you can play the song with few or no mistakes. Then, as your skills improve, increase the tempo until you can play the song at the tempo on the CD.

LESSON 4 | **The Grand Staff**

So far, you've learned to play notes with your right hand and with your left hand separately. Now, it's time to put them together. When the treble and bass clef staves are combined, they form a ***grand staff***. The treble clef is on top, and the bass clef is on the bottom. Bar lines, which separate the measures, extend from the top of the treble to the bottom of the bass clef.

Reading the grand staff will take some time and practice, as you're required to read both treble and bass clef at the same time. Be patient, take your time, and this skill will come along quite naturally. In the next example, you are only required to play from one clef at a time in the first four measures. Then, your left and right hands play in unison for the final two measures. This exercise is designed to familiarize you with moving your eyes back and forth between the two staves. Work slowly and remember to count.

Grand Stuff

Track 16

And now, it's time for your first song using both hands.

Track 17

Try to keep
your eyes on
the music,
instead of
on the
piano.

Rockin' Bells

Introducing the Pickup

Instead of starting a song with a rest, a pickup measure is sometimes used. In a pickup, any opening rests are simply deleted. So, if a pickup has only one beat, you count "one, two, three" and start playing on beat 4.

with rests:

with pickup:

Dem Saints

Let's pull it all together now—quarter notes, half notes, rests, and pickups—all on the grand staff. Take it slowly, and gradually work up to the tempo on the CD.

Under the Shade Tree

You Can Come and Get It

Are you becoming comfortable reading the grand staff? If so, continue to the next section. If you're still having trouble, feel free to practice the songs in this section as often as necessary to improve your reading skills. Using a metronome is especially helpful for developing grand staff reading skills.

Musical Intervals

Up until this point, we've only played single-note lines with either hand. In this lesson, you'll learn to play more than one note simultaneously with either hand. An *interval* is the musical difference between two notes. Take a look at the five notes in C position below.

▶ Play through each interval, noting how each sounds. (Play C, then D; play C, then E; and so on...)

As you can see, the musical spaces between the notes are labeled with numeric intervals. Now, if we rearrange the notes and stack them as we do in "Interval Training" (Track 21), we get something a little more musical.

The Repeat Sign

These are *repeat signs*: . They direct you to repeat everything found between them. If only one sign appears, go back to the beginning of the song and play the music one more time.

Interval Training

Track 21

We Rock Along

Let's try an exercise played in 3rds with both the left and right hands. The fingerings have been marked above the notes for you. As previously, start slowly, count carefully, and feel free to practice each hand separately as well as together until you can play the part up to tempo with the CD.

Third Time's a Charm

The next exercise is arranged in 4ths and 5ths. The first two measures are played with the right hand, and the second two are played with the left.

The Perfect Intervals

Block and Tackle

Movin' and Groovin'

The C Major Chord

Two or more notes played simultaneously constitute a chord, which is made up of intervals. The first full chord we'll play on the piano is the C major chord. The C major chord is a three-note chord, also known as a triad. The three notes of the chord are: C, E, and G.

 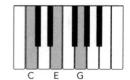

Let's try playing the C major chord with your left and right hands.

Track 27

C to Shining C

Dynamics

When listening to piano performances, you may notice that some are loud, some are quiet, and some are in between. **Dynamics** tell you how loud or soft to play the music. The **p** sign (piano) indicates that the part should be played softly. The *mf* sign (mezzo forte) indicates a moderately loud volume. The *f* sign (forte) directs you to play loudly.

piano	mezzo forte	forte
p	*mf*	*f*
play softly	play moderately loud	play loudly

On the piano, these dynamics are achieved by using normal (mezzo forte), more (forte), or less (piano) force to depress the key.

And now, we'll play our first song using dynamics and the C major chord to accompany the melody.

► This song has a *mf* dynamic marking, so play it with normal force on the keys.

Brother John

Staccato Notes

Some songs require you to play notes in a short, abrupt fashion—separate from the surrounding notes. This technique is called **staccato**. Staccato notes are indicated by a small dot placed above or below the notehead. To play staccato notes on a piano, strike the key and immediately lift your finger off as quickly as possible.

staccato dot

Two to Tangle

Dotted Half Notes

In an earlier chapter, you learned that in 4/4 time, a quarter note receives one beat, a half note receives two beats, and a whole note receives four beats. The **dotted** half note receives **three** beats. The small dot to the right of the notehead tells you to add one half of the note's value to its duration.

Track 30

The Garden Song

3/4 Time Signature

The dotted half note is commonly found in songs that use 3/4 meter, such as the waltz. The 3/4 time signature indicates that the quarter note receives one beat, and that there are three beats per measure.

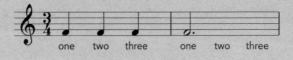

Three Times a Measure

I'll Come Over There

Notes A and B

Left Hand

So far, you've learned about notation, rhythm, intervals, and chords using only the five notes in C position. It's time to add two new notes—A and B. We'll begin with the B note played with the left hand.

The B note occupies the second line on the staff in bass clef. On the piano keyboard, it is located one key to the left of the C note and is played by stretching your left-hand pinky finger over one key while in C position.

B song

Track 33

Staying with the left hand for a moment, let's learn the A note. The A note occupies the top line of the staff in the bass clef. On the keyboard, it is one key to the right of the G note, and is played by stretching your thumb to the right.

A Song

Track 34

Right Hand

In the treble clef, the B note occupies the space below the first ledger line below the staff. It is played by stretching your thumb one key to the left of middle C.

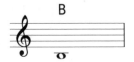

B Song, Part 2

Track 35

► Notice that the final C note is played with finger 2. This is easier then playing two consecutive notes with finger 1.

The A note occupies the second space on the staff in the treble clef. It is played by stretching your right-hand pinky finger one key to the right of G while in C position.

A Song, Part 2

Track 36

F and G7 Chords

Now that you've got the A and B notes under your fingers, you're ready to learn two new chords: F major and G7.

The F major chord contains the notes F, A, and C. It is played with fingers 1, 4, and 5 on your right hand, and with fingers 5, 2, and 1 on your left hand.

The G7 chord contains the notes G, B, and F. It is played with fingers 1, 4, and 5 on your right hand, and with fingers 5, 2, and 1 with your left hand.

C-F-G7 Song

Track 37

Marianne

Ties

A tie is a curved line that connects two notes of the same pitch. They are useful when you need to extend the value of a note across a bar line. When you see a tie, play the first note and then hold it for the total value of both notes.

All Tied Up

Kumbaya

Track 40

This song has a pick-up. Begin playing on beat 3.

The next example contains ties in both the right- and left-hand parts. Counting is extremely important for performing this exercise correctly. Take your time and work up to the tempo on the CD.

Rover Come Home

Track 41

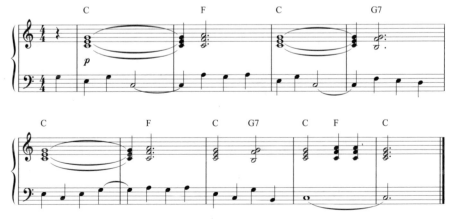

Big Brown Eyes

Eighth Notes

If you divide a quarter note in half, you get an **eighth note**. An eighth note looks like a quarter note, but it has a flag on it.

Two eighth notes equal one quarter note. To help you keep track of the beat, consecutive eighth notes are connected with a beam.

To count eighth notes, say the beat number on the downbeat, and say "and" on the upbeat. Practice this by counting while tapping the rhythm with your foot. The downbeat occurs when your foot hits the floor, and the upbeat is when you raise your foot up to tap again. Once you can tap and count aloud, try playing the notes while counting and tapping.

Track 43

Eight Is Enough

count: 1 and 2 and 3 and 4 and

The next example presents eighth notes in a musical context for both the right and left hands. Be sure to start slowly, as eighth notes move twice as fast as quarter notes.

Track 44

Remember to keep your eyes on the music, not your fingers.

Trading Places

Endings

The next song has a first and second ending. Play the song once to the repeat sign (1st ending), then repeat it from the beginning. The second time through, however, skip the first ending and play the second ending to finish the song.

Track 45

Up a Creek

▶ Don't forget to skip the first ending when you repeat the song.

▶ Watch the fingering in the second ending.

Eighth Rests

If you divide a quarter rest in half, you get two eighth rests. An eighth rest looks a bit like a number "7," but with a curved top (⁊). Count eighth rests in the same manner as eighth notes.

Track 46

Rock 'n' Rest

Track 47

Rumba Rumble

Try counting aloud "one-and-two-and..." to help you play the correct rhythm.

Slurs and Legato

Not to be confused with the tie, a slur is a curved line that connects two or more notes on different lines or spaces of the staff. A slur directs you to smoothly connect the notes of a phrase. Do this by holding down the piano key of the first note in the phrase until the second note is sounded. Then, release the first key. In doing so, the notes flow together seamlessly, a sound known as legato.

Track 48

Followsong

The Slurpy Waltz

Track 49

▶ Note the fingerings in measures 5-8 and 14-15.

Dotted Quarter Notes

When we introduced dotted half notes, you learned that a dot next to the note-head extends the duration of the note by one-half its value. The same can be done with quarter notes. A **dotted quarter note** has a duration equal to a quarter note plus one eighth note.

Track 50

Dotted Quarter Demo

Here is a short song that contains both single notes and chords with dotted quarter-note rhythms.

Dot Matrix

Samba Dot

G Position

It's time to introduce some new, higher notes on the keyboard, achieved with an easy move to the *G position*. From the C position, move your right hand to the right on the keyboard and place your thumb on the G note above middle C (where your pinky finger was formerly placed). Your remaining four fingers then fall on notes A, B, and new notes C and D. The C note occupies the third space on the staff in treble clef, and the D note occupies the fourth line in treble clef.

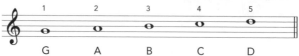

Moving from the C to G position (and back) requires two new techniques: the *cross-over* and the *cross-under*. To change from C to G position, cross your thumb (finger 1) *under* your fingers to the new position at an appropriate place in the music, typically after playing either an E or F note with the third or fourth finger. To return to C position, cross your third or fourth finger *over* the thumb to the appropriate note.

In the next example, as finger 4 plays F, cross your thumb under to play G. In measure 6, as finger 1 plays G, cross finger 4 over to play F.

Track 53

The Keys to Success

Rock the Boat

Broken Chords

When you're playing chords in the left hand, there's no rule that says you have to play all three notes of the chord simultaneously. For a change in feel, you may wish to try **broken chords**. To play broken chords, you will typically first play the lowest note of the chord shape followed by the two higher notes. The next example contains C, F, and G7 chords. For the C chord, first play the low C note, then the E and G together. For F, play the low C note, then F and A together. For G7, first play B, then G and F together.

Break It Up

The Caissons Go Rocking Along

Shifting Positions

When changing positions, it's sometimes necessary to move your entire hand rather than crossing over or under your fingers. Such is the case in "Bach Rock," and these position changes are marked for you.

Bach Rock

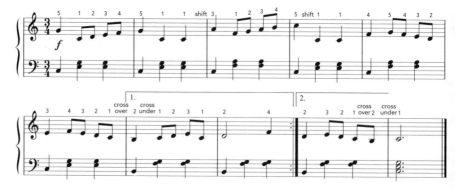

The Major Scale

The major scale is the basic building block of music. A *scale* is an arrangement of notes in specific patterns of half and whole steps. Most scales have eight notes with the top and bottom notes an octave apart. The notes you've learned so far—C, D, E, F, G, A, B—form the C major scale.

To play from C to C with the right hand, start in C position and play the first three notes (C, D, E). Then, perform a cross under to place your thumb on the F note and play the remaining five notes of the scale. To descend the scale, play the first five notes in position, then cross finger 3 over your thumb to play E, and finish the scale with fingers 2 and 1.

Track 58

C Major Scale

With the left hand in C position, play the first five notes in position, then cross finger 3 over to play the A note and finish the scale with fingers 2 and 1. When you descend, play C–B–A, then cross finger 1 under to play the G note. This puts you back into C position.

Track 59

C Major Scale

Joy to the World

Track 61

Let's Climb Together

Practice each hand separately, then put the two parts together.

Until this point, you've only played on the white keys of the piano. The black keys, however, also play an integral role in making music: they sound the sharps and flats.

The Black Keys

A *sharp* note is one half step higher than the original note. Whenever you see a sharp sign (♯) next to a note, play the next key to the right (whether black or white).

A *flat* note is one half step lower than the original note. Whenever you see a flat sign (♭) next to a note, play the next key to the left (whether black or white).

A sharp or flat symbol is only used once on the same note within a measure. That is, if one F has a sharp, then all Fs that follow in that measure are played as F♯. The note value returns to normal in the following measure.

An *enharmonic* is defined as two notes that have the same pitch but are spelled differently. Enharmonic notes are played on the same key. Figure 53 is played entirely on the black keys and contains examples of sharped and flatted notes that form enharmonics.

Track 62

The Black Keys

► To play a black key, use the same finger that would play the nearest white key. For example, in C position, use finger 3 for E♭, finger 4 for F♯, and so on...

Track 63

Sharps and Flats

40

Boogie Blues

rack 64

All Black

rack 65

Remember, a flat sign indicates that the note should be played flat each time it appears within the measure.

New Chords: Am, Dm, E7

It's time to learn three new chords: Am, Dm, and E7. The diagrams below show the fingerings for each of the three chords in both the right and left hand.

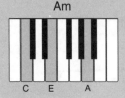

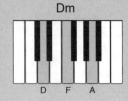

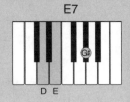

Track 66

New Chords

Track 67

Minor Tom

Damper Pedal

By now, you've probably noticed that there are three foot pedals on your piano. The one on the right is called the damper pedal. When you hold the damper pedal down, any note you sound will continue to ring after you take your finger off the key. Use your right foot to operate the pedal, keeping your heel on the ground at all times, which results in your ankle acting as a sort of hinge.

The sign for using the damper pedal looks like this:

pedal down   pedal up
                            hold pedal

The following song uses broken chords, or arpeggios, in combination with the damper pedal for an almost harp-like quality.

Pedal to the Floor

Even though every note is played with the damper pedal depressed, be sure to depress and release the pedal where indicated to get the proper effect.

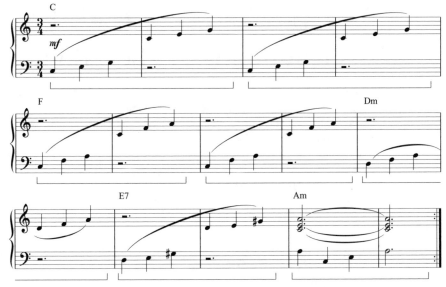

New Bells

Be sure to watch for when the pedal is used.

Notes **D** and **E**

In bass clef, the D note occupies the space above the first ledger line above the staff. The E lies on the second ledger line above the staff.

G Position for the Left Hand

Just as you did with your right hand, you can play in G position with your left hand as well. In G position, finger 5 plays G; finger 4 plays A; finger 3 plays B; finger 2 plays C; and finger 1 plays the new note D and is also responsible for stretching over to play the note E.

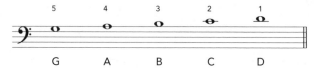

Here's a short exercise for playing D and E with the left hand in G position.

Track 70

D and E Song

C, G, D7 for the Left Hand

You've already learned the C major chord with the C as the lowest note: C–E–G. Regardless of the order in which you play those three notes, however, they still form a C major chord. If you're playing in G position with your left hand, it's easiest to play the chord with the G as the lowest note, like this:

Also in G position, you can play a G major chord.

The D7 chord is also in G position, although you'll need to shift finger 1 down one half step to the F# on the black key to the left of G.

Three Chord Rock

Track 71

Feel free to practice playing these chords in an order different than that written in the example. Look for common tones for which you don't need to move your fingers when changing chords. For example, when switching from G to C, finger 1 plays the low G in both chords.

Goin' to the Fair

Up on the Saddle

Coco Cay

More New Notes

E, F, and G for the Right Hand

The note E is played with either finger 5 of the right hand in G position or with finger 3 of the right hand in C position up one octave. The F and G notes are played with fingers 4 and 5, respectively, in C position one octave higher than previously. In treble clef, E is in the top space of the staff, F is on the top line, and G occupies the space immediately above the staff.

E-F-G Song

Track 75

G and A for the Left Hand

To play the low G and A notes in the bass clef, shift your hand down to the G position below the C position you first learned.

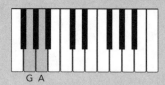

In bass clef, the G note occupies the bottom line of the staff, and the A note takes up the first space.

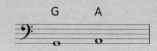

48

G and A Song

Mozart's Musings

*On repeat, play C w/finger 3.

C, G, D7 for the Right Hand

Previously, you learned the C major chord with the C as the lowest note. As with the left hand, the C major chord can also be played with the G as the lowest note.

The G and D7 chords are also played in G position, though you'll have to stretch your thumb down to the F♯ (black key to the left of G) when you play the D7 chord.

As with the left hand, look for common tones when changing chords. This will help the change go much smoother.

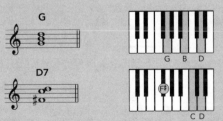

49

Track 78

G-C-D7 Song

Track 79

Country Song

► Note the slurs in the bass clef. Be sure to play with a smooth legato technique.

Track 80

Rock 'n' Funk

► Watch for the moves in the left hand.

Key Signatures

In popular music, there are 12 musical keys. These keys are based on the 12 major scales and the notes contained in each.

G Major

The key of G major contains one sharp: F. In the key of G, a sharp sign is placed on the top line of the staff immediately to the right of the treble clef, or on the fourth line of the staff immediately to the right of the bass clef. This indicates that every time an F appears in the music, you should play F#. Try the G major scale below.

G Major Scale

Track 81

G Major Scale

Track 82

Cha-Cha Pet

Track 83

► Don't forget to play every F note as F#.

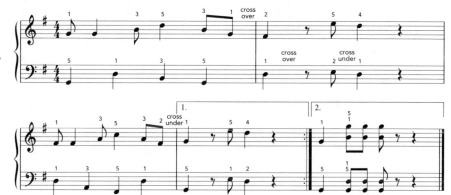

F Major

The key of F major contains one flat: B. In the key of F, a flat sign is placed on the middle line of the staff immediately to the right of the treble clef, or on the second line of the staff immediately to the right of the bass clef. This indicates that every time a B appears in the music, you should play B♭.

Track 84

F Major Scale

Track 85

▶ New note: the low F occupies the space beneath the staff.

F Major Scale

More New Chords: F, B♭, C7

The F, B♭, and C7 chords all belong to the key of F major. The fingerings are given in the diagrams below.

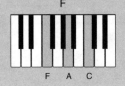

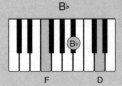

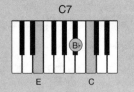

Beetle Song

Practice these chords several times, and change the order to become accustomed to switching between them. When you have them down, try the next song.

Both Ways

Ol' Smokey

▶ In this song, the two beats missing from the pickup measure are found in the last measure of the song.

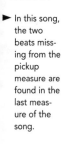

The Natural Sign

The *natural* sign (♮) cancels a sharp or a flat on a note. The note returns to its natural pitch, but only for the measure in which it appears. Often, if the same note appears in the next measure, a **courtesy accidental**—a sharp or flat sign—will appear next to the note to remind you to play it sharp or flat again.

Track 88

Naturally

Track 89

Naturally, Part 2

Track 90

► Note the ♭ sign in measure 5. This is a courtesy accidental, which is used to remind you that the natural sign in the preceeding measure no longer applies.

Nature Class

Technonature

The Grand Finale

The following three arrangements cover many of the lessons you learned in this book, including dynamics, ties, shifts, broken chords, and more.

Amazing Grace

Track 92

Scarborough Fair

New note:
the low A note
in the treble
clef is on the
second ledger
line beneath
the staff.

Chuggin'

▶ Note: Work on the left hand first to achieve a steady rhythm. Play the repeated eighth notes with an alternating 2-3-2-3 fingering.

Bonus Songs

The last section of this book features five well-known pop and rock favorites. Before we begin, let's learn a few new things.

New Chords

If you see a chord you're not familiar with, just remember that it consists of notes you already know. Learn the chord one note at a time, if you need to. Here are a few of the new chords that you'll see:

A **slash chord** is a chord with a note other than the root in the bass.

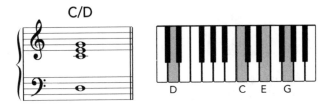

An inversion is another voicing of a chord; the same notes, but a different order. (You learned this Em chord in Level 2, but in a different inversion.)

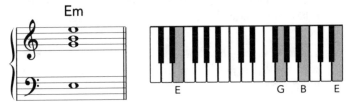

A **sixth chord** contains the 6th above the root note, sometimes in place of the 5th.

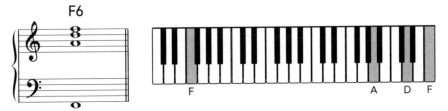

A minor seventh chord is a minor triad with an added 7th.

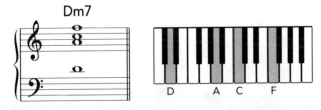

Multi-Measure Rests

Rather than writing out many measures of rest in a row, a shorthand notation is often used with the number of measures rest written in above a multi-measure rest symbol. Multi-measure rests often appear at the start of a song, before the keyboard enters.

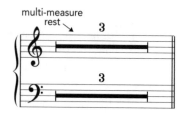

Fermata, Ritard, D.S. (𝄋), and Fine

A *fermata* symbol (⌢) above a note or chord indicates a hold or a pause. This is typically found at the end of a song.

A *ritard* indicates a gradual slowing of the tempo, again usually at the end of the piece.

The indication D.S. (dal segno) means "from the sign." If you see it above the staff, return to the sign (𝄋) earlier in the song and resume playing from there.

The indication *al Fine* means "to the end." If you see it after the indication D.S., return to the sign (𝄋) earlier in the song and resume playing until you see the word *Fine*.

Takin' Care of Business

Words and Music by Randy Bachman

Track 95

Interlude

Wonderful Tonight

Words and Music by Eric Clapton

Save the
Last Dance for Me

Words and Music by Doc Pomus and Mort Shuman

Additional Lyrics

2. Oh, I know that the music's fine
   Like a sparkling wine; go and have your fun.
   Laugh and sing, but while we're apart
   Don't give your heart to anyone.

3. You can dance, go and carry on
   Till the night is gone and it's time to go.
   If he asks if you're all alone,
   Can he take you home, you must tell him no.

Limbo Rock

Words and Music by Billy Strange and Jon Sheldon

Additional Lyrics

3. First you spread your limbo feet,
   Then you move to limbo beat
   Limbo ankle, limbo knee;
   Bend back, like the limbo tree
   To Chorus

4. La, la, la, la, la, la, la... etc.
   (Cont. through Chorus)

5. Get yourself a limbo girl,
   Give that chick a limbo whirl
   There's a limbo moon above
   You will fall in limbo love.
   To Chorus

Track 99

Y.M.C.A.

Words and Music by Jacques Morali,
Henri Belolo and Victor Willis

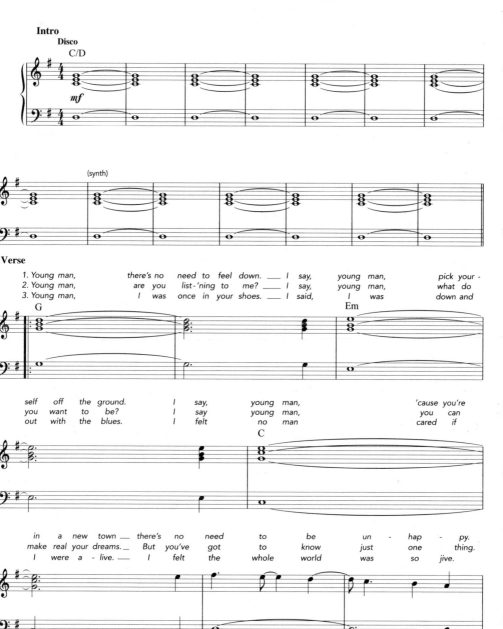

Verse

1. Young man, there's no need to feel down. ___ I say, young man, pick your-
2. Young man, are you list-'ning to me? ___ I say, young man, what do
3. Young man, I was once in your shoes. ___ I said, I was down and

self off the ground. I say, young man, 'cause you're
you want to be? I say young man, you can
out with the blues. I felt no man cared if

in a new town ___ there's no need to be un - hap - py.
make real your dreams. ___ But you've got to know just one thing.
I were a - live. ___ I felt the whole world was so jive.

Play Today!

The Ultimate Self-Teaching Method

Have you always wanted to make music? Help has arrived in the *Play Today!* series! These fabulous book/CD packs are a beginner's complete guide to the basics. Available for a wide variety of instruments, they feature easy-to-understand lessons, a revolutionary "teacher on CD" that actually talks you through how each example should sound, plus lots of popular songs that let you put your new musical knowledge to the test! Listen and learn at your own pace, in the comfort of your own home. You'll be amazed at what you can teach yourself!

PLAY GUITAR TODAY! – LEVEL 1

Teaches: chords and riffs; picking and strumming; playing tips and techniques; standard notation and tablature; and much more! Includes many examples on CD, and 5 fantastic songs: Brown Eyed Girl • Every Breath You Take • Let It Be • Time Is on My Side • Wild Thing.
_____00842055 Book/CD Pack......................................$14.95 ISBN # 0-634-03052-3

PLAY BASS TODAY! – LEVEL 1 • *by Chris Kringel*

Teach yourself bass the easy way! This method covers: riffs and scales; all musical styles; playing tips and techniques; how to read standard notation and tablature; and much more. Songs: I Saw Her Standing There • My Girl • Walk Don't Run • Wild Thing • Wonderful Tonight.
_____00698997 Book/CD Pack......................................$14.95 ISBN # 0-634-03299-2

PLAY DRUMS TODAY! – LEVEL 1 • *by Scott Schroedl*

This ultimate self-teaching method for drums can be used by students who want to teach themselves, or by teachers for private or group study. Offers instruction on: beats, songs and fills; all musical styles; playing tips and techniques; music notation; and more. Songs: Friends in Low Places • The House Is Rockin' • I Saw Her Standing There • Never Gonna Let You Go • What I Like About You.
_____00699001 Book/CD Pack......................................$14.95 ISBN # 0-634-03300-X

PLAY PIANO TODAY! – LEVEL 1 • *by Warren Wiegratz*

The perfect series to help you start playing piano today! This book/CD pack will teach the absolute beginner all the basics, plus how to play 5 great songs: Friends in Low Places • The House Is Rockin' • Takin' Care of Business • Wonderful Tonight • Y.M.C.A..
_____00699044 Book/CD Pack......................................$14.95 ISBN # 0-634-03301-8

PLAY FLUTE TODAY! – LEVEL 1

A fabulous pack for the beginning flutist, this book/CD pack teaches all the essentials, and lets players progress at their own pace! The CD includes audio instruction as well as demo tracks for the exercises complete with background accompaniments. Songs: Chariots of Fire • Forrest Gump – Main Title (Feather Theme) • The Man from Snowy River (Main Title Theme) • Rock & Roll – Part II (The Hey Song) • We Will Rock You.
_____00699489 Book/CD Pack......................................$14.95 ISBN # 0-634-03327-1

PLAY CLARINET TODAY! – LEVEL 1

A terrific tutor for the beginning clarinetist, this book/CD pack teaches all the basics of playing, and 5 hit songs: Chariots of Fire • Forrest Gump – Main Title (Feather Theme) • The Man from Snowy River (Main Title Theme) • Rock & Roll – Part II (The Hey Song) • We Will Rock You.
_____00699490 Book/CD Pack......................................$14.95 ISBN # 0-634-03329-8

PLAY ALTO SAX TODAY! – LEVEL 1

Learn to play the alto saxophone at your own pace! This book/CD pack walks you through the basics, and teaches you to play 5 songs: Chariots of Fire • Forrest Gump – Main Title (Feather Theme) • The Man from Snowy River (Main Title Theme) • Rock & Roll – Part II (The Hey Song) • We Will Rock You.
_____00699492 Book/CD Pack......................................$14.95 ISBN # 0-634-03331-X

PLAY TRUMPET TODAY! – LEVEL 1

Take up the trumpet today! This book/CD pack makes it easier than ever before, taking beginners through all the essentials, then teaching them 5 top songs to practice and play: Chariots of Fire • Forrest Gump – Main Title (Feather Theme) • The Man from Snowy River (Main Title Theme) • Rock & Roll – Part II (The Hey Song) • We Will Rock You.
_____00699491 Book/CD Pack......................................$14.95 ISBN # 0-634-03330-1